Life As ...

Life As an Engineer on the First Railroads in America

Kate Shoup

Cavendish Square
New York

Published in 2016 by Cavendish Square Publishing, LLC
243 5th Avenue, Suite 136, New York, NY 10016

Website: cavendishsq.com

This publication represents the opinions and views of the author based on his or her personal experience, knowledge, and research. The information in this book serves as a general guide only. The author and publisher have used their best efforts in preparing this book and disclaim liability rising directly or indirectly from the use and application of this book.

CPSIA Compliance Information: Batch #CW16CSQ

All websites were available and accurate when this book was sent to press.

Library of Congress Cataloging-in-Publication Data

Shoup, Kate, 1972- author.
Life as an engineer on the first railroads in America / Kate Shoup.
pages cm. — (Life as...)
Includes bibliographical references and index.
ISBN 978-1-5026-1089-8 (hardcover) ISBN 978-1-5026-1088-1 (paperback) ISBN 978-1-5026-1090-4 (ebook)
1. Railroads—United States—History—Juvenile literature. 2. Locomotive engineers—United States—History—Juvenile literature. I. Title. II. Title: First railroads in America.
TF23.S56 2016
385.0973—dc23

2015023779

Editorial Director: David McNamara
Editor: Kristen Susienka
Copy Editor: Nathan Heidelberger
Art Director: Jeffrey Talbot
Designer: Joseph Macri
Senior Production Manager: Jennifer Ryder-Talbot
Production Editor: Renni Johnson
Photo Research: J8 Media

The photographs in this book are used by permission and through the courtesy of: Library of Congress, cover; Peter Newark American Pictures/Bridgeman Images, 5; Lebrecht Music and Arts Photo Library/Alamy, 6; National Archives/File:1869-Golden Spike.jpg/Wikimedia Commons, 9; Denver Public Library, Western History Collection/Bridgeman Images, 10; Public Domain/File:Casey Jones.jpg/Wikimedia Commons, 13; Chicago History Museum/Getty Images, 14; North Wind Picture Archives, 17; Stephen Barnes/Public Transport/Alamy, 19; FloridaStock/Shutterstock.com, 20; Library of Congress, 21, 24; PhotoQuest/Getty Images, 22; FPG/Getty Images, 23, Artem Furman/Shutterstock.com, 27.

Printed in the United States of America

Contents

Introduction

America's first railroads were built in 1828, on the East Coast. Soon, they stretched from New York to California. Railroads changed America. More people moved west. Goods could be shipped more quickly and cheaply. Perhaps most importantly, railroads brought Americans together.

Thousands of men worked on the railroads. Some laid tracks. Some built bridges and tunnels. Some worked in train stations. Some, like the railroad **engineer**, worked on the trains themselves.

The railroad engineer drove the train. He made sure the train arrived safely and on time. People respected and admired railroad engineers. They were very important to the railroad's history.

A train leaves the railroad depot in La Grande, Oregon.

This illustration shows the interior of a carriage on the B&O railroad.

Chapter 1

Railroads Start

One of the first railroads in the United States was called the Baltimore and Ohio (B&O). It was built in 1828. At first, the B&O ran only 13 miles (20.9 kilometers), from Baltimore to Ellicott Mills, Maryland. Later, it stretched hundreds of miles from New York to Illinois. Soon, other railroads were built to connect cities all across the eastern United States.

One important railroad was the Pacific Railroad. It was built by the Central Pacific Railroad Company (CPRR) and the Union Pacific Railroad Company (UPRR) in the mid-1800s. Two groups built the railroad. Workers for the CPRR began in Sacramento, California, and worked east. Workers for the UPRR started in Council Bluffs, Iowa, and moved west. From Council

Bluffs, the Pacific Railroad connected to existing railroads. These went all the way to the Atlantic Ocean. Workers joined the two sets of tracks on May 10, 1869. To celebrate, they held a special ceremony.

Later, workers extended the Pacific Railroad to the San Francisco Bay. The Pacific Railroad was 1,907 miles (3,069 km) long. After it was built, people could travel safely from New York to California in just eight days. Before the railroads, the same trip took six months.

The Pacific Railroad Act

In 1862, the US **Congress** passed the Pacific Railroad Act. It was signed into law by President Abraham Lincoln and allowed for the creation of the Pacific Railroad.

Workers celebrate after the completion of the Pacific Railroad.

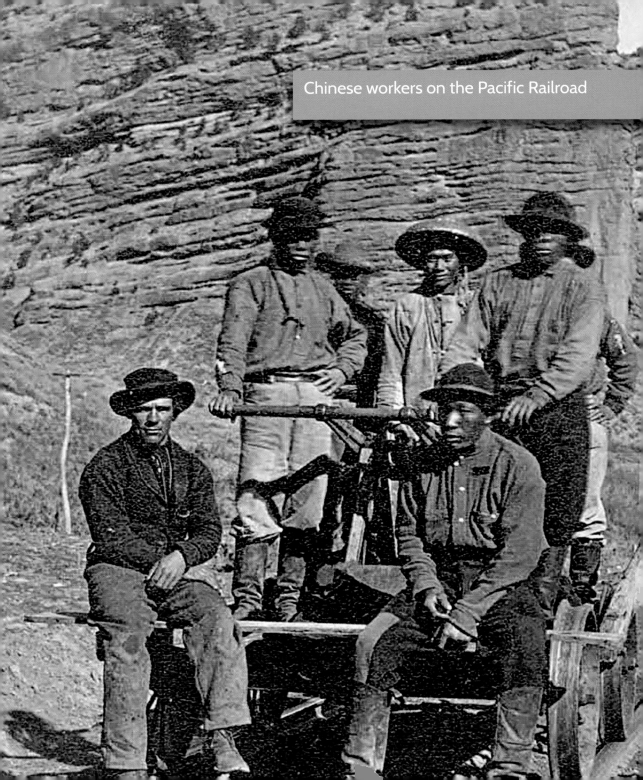

Chinese workers on the Pacific Railroad

Chapter 2

Working on Trains

It takes many workers to build a railroad. Some decide what route the railroad will follow. Some lay the tracks. Some build bridges and tunnels for the railroad to pass over or move through. Some build train stations.

Chinese Workers

Thousands of workers helped build the Pacific Railroad. Many of these workers were from China. Most spent their days high up in the Sierra Nevada Mountains. The work they did was very difficult and dangerous. Workers earned $28 per month (about $400 in 2015).

After the railroad is built, still more workers are needed. Some workers stay at the train station to sell tickets to passengers and help carry bags. Others work on the trains. For example, the train conductor collects tickets from passengers and makes sure the train runs on time.

Perhaps the most important person is the engineer, who drives the train. Most engineers on America's first railroads learned how to drive trains during the Civil War. Trains were used to move soldiers from one place to another.

Casey Jones: Hero Engineer

John Luther "Casey" Jones was a famous railroad engineer. He drove a train for the Illinois Central Railroad. Once, Jones saw a little girl on the tracks less than 200 feet (61 meters) in front of his train. He ran to the front of the engine car, climbed onto the **cowcatcher**, and pulled the girl to safety. In 1900, Jones's train crashed into another train that was stuck on the tracks. Instead of jumping from his train before the crash, Jones stayed on board to try to slow it down. He was killed. However, thanks to Jones, none of the passengers on the train were badly hurt. He is considered a hero.

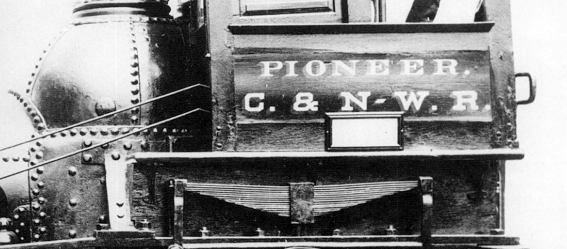
An engineer manning a steam engine

Chapter 3

Daily Life

The main job of a railroad engineer was to drive the train. First, however, he had to get the train moving.

Most of the early trains had steam engines. To run the train, the crew burned coal in a furnace. This boiled water in a nearby tank called a boiler. The boiling water made steam. As the steam built up, pressure caused **pistons** in the engine to move. This powered the train's wheels. The engineer could then drive the train. He used a **throttle** to control the flow of steam into the pistons. To stop the train, he used a brake.

When the train approached a hill, the crew burned more coal. This added power, but they had to be careful. If they burned too much coal, the train might go too fast. This could cause the train to crash.

To warn people of the train's approach, the engineer used a steam whistle. Many engineers created their own whistling patterns. Often, people who lived near the tracks could tell which engineer was passing just by the sound of the whistle.

For most of the ride, the engineer sat in the engine room and watched the tracks ahead. He looked for signals, which might warn him of a stalled train or another problem ahead. He also watched for obstacles, such as cows on the tracks. The engineer stopped the train at stations along the route. There, the train dropped off passengers and picked up new ones. Train cars containing supplies might also be added or removed.

Usually, the trip was smooth. Sometimes, however, things went wrong. A train could be delayed or break down. Storms arose. Even when faced with these problems, the engineer had to make sure the train arrived safely at its destination.

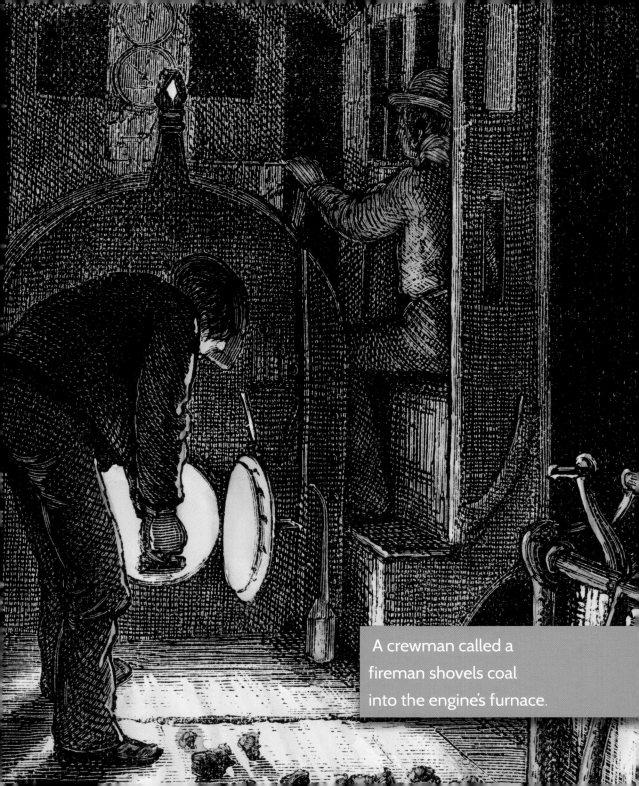

A crewman called a fireman shovels coal into the engine's furnace.

An engineer's schedule on board a train might look like this:

Task 1	Load the coal
Task 2	Fill the water tank
Task 3	Oil the pistons
Task 4	Connect the train cars to the engine
Task 5	Stoke the coal
Task 6	Build up steam
Task 7	Release the brake
Task 8	Move the throttle
Task 9	Leave the station
Task 10	Blow the whistle
Task 11	Drive the train
Task 12	Watch for signals and obstacles
Task 13	Ease the train into the next station

A steam engine's controls

A steam train runs through the Rocky Mountains.

Chapter 4

Tools of the Trade

Railroad engineers used many tools. One was the engine itself. On America's first railroads, each engineer was assigned his own engine. He kept it oiled and polished. He even chose what color to paint it.

The engine contained other tools inside. One was the pressure gauge. It showed how much pressure there was in the boiler. If the pressure in the boiler got too high, the train could blow up. If the engineer noticed there was too much pressure, he released some through a special opening called a valve.

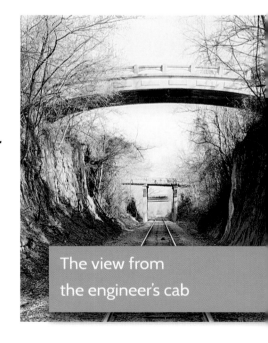

The view from the engineer's cab

The telegraph was an important invention.

Most train tracks were **single-track**. To make sure trains did not collide, railroads followed a strict schedule. To stay on schedule, the engineer, conductor, **stationmaster**, and other workers used a railroad chronometer. This was a special watch that kept the time.

One important tool for railroads was the telegraph. It was used to send messages from station to station. Messages were sent in **Morse code**. One station might send a message to another station saying a train was running late. Another message might warn of a train stopped on the tracks. Station workers could share this information with the engineer on an oncoming train by displaying signals along the track or at a station. At first, hand signals were used. Later, station workers used mechanical signs.

A worker adjusts the clock at a train station.

Standard Time

Before railroads, each town used its own system to keep track of time. When railroads were created, this made it difficult to maintain railroad schedules. It also caused accidents. In 1853, two trains in New England collided because railroad workers had set different times on their watches. Fourteen people died. Finally, in 1883, American railroads adopted standard time, which created four time zones from coast to coast. This made all the time in specific regions the same. It was no longer difficult for trains to run on schedule. In 1918, standard time became the law of the land.

Passengers board a train in California.

Chapter 5

Why Railroads Are Important

Railroads and railroad engineers had a big effect on America. They brought more people to the western United States. New towns and businesses sprang up.

The railroads didn't just move people quickly and cheaply. They also moved goods such as meat, grain, and vegetables to people all across the country. Thanks to special cold train cars, the goods did not spoil. Suddenly, a person in New York could eat an orange grown in California—in the middle of winter! Railroads also improved mail service. Before, it cost several dollars to mail a letter. After, it cost pennies. Thanks to railroads, people could also stay in touch with loved ones, even if they lived far away.

Most importantly, railroads brought Americans together. In 1869, a *New York Times* article about the Pacific Railroad said, "The inhabitants of the Atlantic seaboard and the dwellers on the Pacific slopes are henceforth ... one people." Today, railroads continue to move supplies and people in the United States and around the world.

A modern high-speed train

Glossary

Congress The government organization that makes laws.

cowcatcher A metal frame at the front of a train that pushes aside cows or other obstacles on the track.

engineer A person who drives and takes care of a train.

Morse code A code that uses clicks and tones to send messages via telegraph.

piston A moving part in a locomotive engine that powers the turning of the wheels.

single-track A railroad line that only has one set of train tracks for trains to run on in both directions.

stationmaster A person who runs a train station.

throttle A mechanism in a train that controls the flow of steam into the pistons.

Find Out More

Books

Alber, Christopher. *Casey Jones and His Railroad Legacy*. New York: Cavendish Square, 2014.

Atkinson, Sam, Jemima Dunne, and Kathryn Hennessy, eds. *Train: The Definitive Visual History*. London, England: DK Publishing, 2014.

Renehan, Edward J., Jr. *The Transcontiental Railroad: The Gateway to the West*. Milestones in American History. New York: Chelsea House Publishers, 2007.

Website

Kids Discover: Trains

www.kidsdiscover.com/spotlight/trains-for-kids

Video

History: Transcontinental Railroad

www.history.com/topics/inventions/transcontinental-railroad/videos

Index

About the Author

Kate Shoup has written more than thirty books and has edited hundreds more. When not working, Kate loves to watch IndyCar racing, ski, read, and ride her motorcycle. She lives in Indianapolis with her husband, her daughter, and their dog. To learn more about Kate and her work, visit www.kateshoup.com.